Life L and Lyrical Translations of My Soul

A collection of poems
by Kiah Morris
2020

Edited by James Lawton

Cover art by Kiah Morris © 2020 (mixed media, collage)

Life Lessons and Lyrical Translations of My Soul. Copyright © 2020 by Kiah Morris. All rights reserved. Printed in the United States of America. No part of this book may be used or reproduced in any manner whatsoever without written permission except in the case of brief quotations embodied in critical articles or review.

Acknowledgments

I need to thank so many people, many of whom have no idea how much they have influenced my writing and creative art.

- My mother for seeing my gifts and pressing me to pursue them, even when my introversion wanted to convince me otherwise. Her sacrifices to get me the lessons and opportunities I had are incalculable.
- My sister Jamillah for sharing with me her first published poem, printed in a middle-school literary journal. I still remember stanzas from those pieces which showed a vulnerability and humor that clearly impacts my work today.
- My sister C. Zawadi for introducing me to spoken word, the power of oration and the deep roots of oral history and performance.
- My father for sharing your father's beautiful volumes of poetry.
- James for giving me our beautiful son, the love of my life; your support and loving care of this work.
- My dear friend Shane for putting pen to paper again and again to capture our poetic journey.
- The standard-bearers of transformative spoken word, Jaquanda and Jacinda for raising a generation of poets and prophets who are changing the world.
- My funk family: Nicki, John, Sam, Nathan, Adam, Joe, David, Bill, Jake, Linda, Kim; I found my voice again with you all.
- Matt and the gents at Akin Studios for believing in this work 100%.
- And those I have loved, lost, met, danced with and made art. The best is yet to come.

Preface

Friends, this collection of poems is my first foray into publishing my work.

These poems are poignant, dark, funny, inspirational and deeply personal. Non-traditional, sometimes prose-like. Not all are appropriate for all audiences and some may trigger deep emotions.

Included are poems about my heartbreaks, my triumphs and the ups and downs of my life. Sharing these stories and my art is an incredibly vulnerable act, and well worth it.

Themes came forth from this work:

Inspiration and Laughter – Poems that explore the challenges of marathon-esque journeys, resilience and rather clumsy sexual themes.
Helpless Romanticism – I love, love. I get sappy and emotional at times.
Love Letters – This is a growing series of pieces inspired by a friendship that began in my youth and spans decades of memories.
Through the Darkness and Into the Light – Pieces that talk about misogyny, violence and the human spirit. This includes special poems I wrote during my trip to Central America with Oxfam, one of which was entered into the Congressional Record.
I Got Ex Issues – Break ups. Heartbreak. Letting go.
The Politics of American Racism – Title says it all.
Spirituality Manifested – The ways I use my gifts as a healer, intuit and human to express my spirituality.

I hope that you will enjoy this collection, and perhaps be inspired to create your own.

Table of Contents

Acknowledgments 3
Preface 4
Bloom 8
Welfare Politician 9
On Becoming a Marathoner 18
Sisterhood 27
What Channing Tatum Taught Me About Beatlemania 28
Fargo 37
All I Have to Give to You 44
It's Not Enough 46
Reveal 48
First Blush 51
Subtext and Secrets 53
Angel 57
Anthem 60
I Saw The Places They Died 70
For Clementina, La Lenca 74
Choosing Battles 75
Heart Chakra 81
Redemptive Entry 82
The Shadows Reflected In My Pupils 87
AA_NA 90
When Picket Fences Feel More Like Barbed Wire Barricades 94
Bleached Bloodlines 97
Meant for the Slaughter 98

Respectability Politics 99
Exponential Love 102
Greatness 110
Kaleidoscopic Transferrence 111
Natural Giver 112
About the Author 114

Inspiration & Laughter

Bloom

Just when I start to feel the world around me is crumbling, decaying, self-destructing and irreversibly spiraling towards insanity or perpetual despair, my Aloe plant starts to bloom again almost overnight/seriously overcrowded in its decorative but constricting plastic pot quite possibly overwatered and most probably over-nourished/it defies logic in its survival against my uneducated care plans and thrives in spite of the negativity of the outside world/its prickly leaves guard a succulent healing center with a purpose older than time itself/deep green pointed fingers spread haphazardly to touch sunlight wherever it falls/without fail, my Aloe plant teaches lessons in repelling the worst and transforming the chaotic energy of our modern lives to produce charming, delicate, bouquets of pink paradise in stark defiance of our tragic messiness

Welfare Politician

Dusty boxes of nondescript food
Cockroaches crawling
Falling from cracks in the ceiling
Into cereal stench of death and decay
Sadness of urban infrastructure
Crumbling all around us
It was not just another day
Average life in America
For my family this was our everyday reality
We ate lima beans from cans and cream of wheat
and sometimes if we had extra money we might eat
Wheaties the breakfast of champions
Mother wanted us to grow up strong and capable
so that we would not have to continue to live in the
Ghettos of Chicago

We left, but life would be hard
A difficult road where the difference between those
who have and have not was glaring
When you have to have special meal tickets to eat
the same cafeteria food lunch as all your peers but
no one else has to and they can get ice cream with
their pizzas
Where you can't buy the latest clothing

If you are able to get that designer pair of jeans
It is the one purchase you get for the next three years of your life
So you better not gain weight and make sure they fit just right and don't get holes in the knees or anywhere else for that matter
Where two generations of hand-me-downs were such a regular thing

This may sound like a typical middle to lower-class American experience
But don't get it twisted
It was a painful life because the pains of poverty hurt at the soul
When as a parent cannot give your child everything that you would like for them to have
When you bounce rent checks and float power bills to be able to get milk
Because we go through it so fast
To be able to buy eggs because a dozen really doesn't feed that many
And you get really, really crafty in creating ways to make beans and rice into a masterpiece that every child will like.
Well maybe not like, but they have no choice but to eat it anyway

That deadly work ethic that requires you work twice as hard and long as everyone else
That ability to make a dollar out of 15¢

That insistence on survival in a world designed for your resignation and death is something that I never knew how much I would need as an adult

One day I was to learn all about dumpster diving and how perfectly good produce was thrown into metal bins outside the grocery stores in Seattle Because it was not perfect enough for the wealthy to purchase, natural blemishes deemed unsightly. Stashed away, someone's labor tossed aside Someone's food junked.

This punk rock kid with a mohawk named Zen who lived down the hallway from me in a
Tenement slum
A converted whore house where we had one toilet and one shower that we shared with the whole floor. Zen would show me his tricks.
How to survive if you had to because you have no other choice

In that building, I learned from drug dealers, would-be hackers, stripper single moms, pimps, hitchhikers, squatters, sex workers, and anarchists. Each person taught me something new about survival against the odds.
Showed me what real hustle looks like

Years later, I would go to some professional development training somewhere
The only black person in the room
A training on the "culture of poverty"
They gave us an assessment to see if we knew how to survive, where to go for help.
Where are the local grocery dumpsters that are unlocked?
If the shelter was full, could you find a safe place to squat for the night?
Where were the free clothing closets?
A pop quiz about my everyday lessons
I got a perfect score. No one else in the room did

I went back to college and got my degree
The most untraditional of non-traditional students, college wasn't just something to do
The space between existential crises of youth and adulthood, it was real dollars and cents out of my

pocket that I knew I would have to pay back to get where I wanted to be
I took full advantage of the opportunities afforded
International travel, mentoring from legends in the field
And graduated with nothing.
Unable to find work for nearly two years
At the height of the great recession
Terrified about eviction
Many a meal missed to save wherever I could

Fast forward to a new life, starting at the bottom again
How many poor are required to start again, and again and make something from nothing?
Working 50 – 60 hours in a depressed local economy
To make less than I did in the years before college
Now with a baby to care for
I found myself looking for assistance from the state
You know one of those lowlifes that we hear about
Who takes from the government
Uses up all of our benefits and sends our taxes through the roof?
That was me
I was working

Hard all along
But not making enough
And to return to the workforce full-time
To become one of those "productive members of society"
Meant leaving behind my precious child, to see him for but a few waking hours each day,
Paying for needed childcare
But cost was crushing to the tune of
$200 or more a week kind of crushing
So we needed things like childcare subsidy and food stamps to give us some cushion so we didn't have to pay out quite as much out each week out of our small salaries
Save what little we would, like responsible adults are supposed to do.
Here is the twist though,
As we tried to crawl ourselves out of this hole
Out of this pit of poverty
Out of this strain of being broke,
We were punished for trying to ascend to a higher plane
We would reach what they call this cliff, which felt more like crushing weight upon us.
This
Cliff
This cliff

Where by fulfilling the social contract of public benefits
By getting more education
By completing the agreement of taking on even more work than you could bear
Agreeing to even more hours away from your family to make ends meet
You were mercilessly cut off
At one point, I made $50 too much a month to deserve healthcare
It was a reminder, that for the working poor, your work has no real value,
Your strides are unimportant and you deserve nothing but the least for failing to embody American exceptionalism.

But I press on
My community notices my strength and tenacity
My passion in standing up for others every day
They ask me to represent them
The people of my community
The folks in the trailer parks
The ones with no teeth. The friends I make at the laundromat
The ones I meet in state-mandated support groups

They send me up to work in a building where the dome is literally gilded in gold
This space of power, privilege and wealth.
Because of my truth and their truths, I can be a voice of the people
Drive policy and tell real truths and real stories to decision-makers whose lives bear no resemblance
To my own
To those politicos who have never been truly tested
Understand, that I was not wealthy from the $12,000 a year I was given to serve
I am not retired with a nest egg that allowed me to be in that space with cushion
I still counted pennies and rationed many a meal
I served at great sacrifice to my family who had to deal with less of everything, including my presence
But I did it because someone must change things and I was chosen for that moment

So when they callously say, "We must cut these pathetic entitlements"
I remind them of my story
I remind them of the roaches
I remind them that I am the product of public housing
I remind them that those food stamps put food in my child's belly

I remind them

I scream

I speak

I stomp

I fight for the people

Because it is not merely about welfare

The system has never been fair

On Becoming a Marathoner

26.2 miles 26.2 miles 26.2 miles

This was the goal that my sister and I set for ourselves that which we would accomplish.

We knew that we had it within us both as former track runners,
She would be the Olympic level Track Star
Me as the child who was forced to run even though she hated it.
We saw Oprah do it and said "You know what? If she can, then we can too."
So we began our long goal of training to become a part of that elite group of finishers.
Such a grueling process waking at the crack of dawn to run miles before the workday.
Leaving the warmth of my bed for the cruel, dark cold of the morning. And I am not a morning person.
Quality Friday night parties were forgone to make room for long runs on Saturday
Week after week, 20 to 30 miles of pavement on our petite frames.

I got hit by a car once on mile 8 of a 14-mile day. The impact filled me with so much adrenaline and rage that I banged my fists upon the hood of the car, screamed profanities at the driver to the top of my lungs and kept running all the way home.
The pain hit me once I stopped moving. But I persisted.
Days upon days of icing sore legs underneath my desk at work
On those beautiful summer days in Seattle
Runs down breathtaking wooded trails and pristine waterfront shorelines first required passage through the downtown district
And the sight of happy, carefree, well-rested people in beer gardens sipping their craft brews while I had another 16 more miles to go was a bit much.

One training day that began at 4:30 in the morning ended some hours later with a station wagon filled with smiling faces pressed against windows, creeping along the road beside me.
I waited for jeers and pointed fingers at my form or what I am sure was a very unflattering appearance. Drenched in sweat, trudging along, almost a shuffle, nothing at all like the models in Runners World magazine.

Instead they rolled down their windows and cheered. I was stunned.
The driver said, "We just wanted you to know that we saw you running a few hours ago
It is inspiring to see you haven't quit."
I actually
got
misty at the thought
And it wasn't just because I was running uphill or because my thighs were rightfully on fire.

By the time race day came I was terrified, ready and excited
4 1/2 hours of running
We stood at the starting line, a sea of thousands sharing the same goal.
Our friends, our family, eager to celebrate our triumph.
I had 26.2 miles to get through so I jogged along
My legs were tired but they were ready
My feet were burning but they were into it
All I had to do was keep my brain going for 26 miles.
Have you ever tried that before?

To go on foot from one part of a city to Chinatown and across the highway bridge, to Little Italy, the Southside and more?
Seeing cars below and knowing that there are no rides home.
You are in it until the end. It is complete lunacy. I swear.
By mile 10, I had found my groove.
There were so many people, calling out our names, coaching from the sidelines, "Go Kiah, you can do it!"
The crowds were amazing, music, dj's and dancing people, Elvis impersonators. You name it.
I knew I could do this, 26.2
26 .2
26 .2
Then I hit mile 16.
By that point, I no longer wanted any part of it
I just wanted to go home - this was too much, I was bored with the challenge, I was beyond uncomfortable, I was tired
It was insane to press on
My sister somewhere far ahead leapt to a faster pace, I knew I would have to finish alone or not at all

Mile 20, when the adrenaline kicks in is where you get that "runner's high"
But alive is not how I felt
I felt defeated by exhaustion and overwhelmed at the thought of continuance
It seemed like it would never end
I was being outpaced by this ragtag team that wore cowboy hats and pulled over to chug a Budweiser every few miles or so.
These drunk asses were outpacing me. How deflating.
The tears of resignation start to well and it became tempting to halt my momentum and allow the emotions, the doubt to take hold
That's all I wanted to do, maybe just a pause for a moment
Hey, I had tried and that counts right?
But see I'm the kind of person that if I don't get out of bed
I won't get out of bed and the day will pass and my pajamas will have been the only thing that I have worn
But the day before, I boarded a plane to come do this crazy thing
And today, I got up early and put on my lucky Supergirl shirt
And some comfy bottoms

And through this work, they were all wet with the products of effort and stamina.
My eyes, cheeks and neck crystalized in layers of salty sweat
Somehow, I keep going. I keep going.
In an industrial part of the south side
Beautiful little black girls with yarn ribbons in their hair and matching cheerleading outfits
Erupt in cries of encouragement as I pass by
I hear one of them say
"Look at that lady with the 'S' on her chest,"
And my heart bursts
And again, I get misty
I know I must complete this journey

And as I reached the final miles, I cross paths with an elderly man
Moving slowly, but steadily
Who says to me with a knowing smile, "We are going to finish this,
Aren't we young lady?"
And I look into his eyes with gratitude and say, "Yes sir,
Yes, we are."

And like that, it is done. The medal draped on my neck. Beer placed in my hand. Silver blanket draped on my shoulders like a superheroes' cape.

■■

Years later, I find myself at the starting line of a new journey
Having accomplished more than I thought possible,
Can I overcome newly minted mental fears
And treat each new challenge like a marathon that I must complete?
My overly sensitive
Sensitivity to the world's pain drove me to distraction when considering the effect that was sure to
follow
A leader
Plucked from visibility
Leaving others to worry about their own vulnerability
If those who are good can be silenced
What hope is there to find their own pathway to resilience
I look at my circle of women who carry accomplishments greater than those most will ever know
And do not believe I belong

I worry much in my everyday conversations about my ability to show up as one of them
To carry the power of my ancestral mothers to present self-assurance, grace, wisdom and love
My words fumble and fall. My face carries pain and stress of personal burdens
The kind of life challenges that make many crumble under the weight
Will I emerge?
Will I sing again? And if I do find my voice, who will be there to listen?
Others encourage me. They speak words of security. Describing me as I would like to see myself.
I would like to run for miles today
Long and hard, until my lungs ache and my legs collapse
Body quivering, unsure of when and if I will rest
Careening down windy wooded roads, alongside babbling streams
My feet carving paths through mountaintops
My mind memorizing every vista and majestic beauty I pass along the way
Heavy breaths offering prayers of gratitude for the journey
Wet body purified by the sweet release of salty sweat

Kissed by the sun, tanned in a baptismal glow
My muscles are toned and strong and ready
To carry the weight of my life's work
But if I stop at the start of an ascent
Resign at the first twinges of discomfort
Consciously self-sabotage through ill-preparedness
Ignore the messages strewn across the skies
I may never truly know
How very far I might have gone
Nor seen who may have been following in my footsteps all along
I find my legs. I find my breath.
I reach inward and upward, twisting my spirit outward to accept the sunshine
I hear the voices of my sisters pushing me.
Welcoming me in and sending me off into the world!
I find healing. I find solace. I find my voice.
Through this journey, I find myself.
In 26.2 miles, I found a roadmap to always come back to center,
Persevere and find myself.

Sisterhood

The words were simple and they spilled
From my trembling lips with an exhale
Of respite and communication that required no
dissection or expounding for clarity
We heard without the crowding of words
As our arms cradled our hearts
The bottoms of my lids fell heavy with aching tears
I sank into her smile and let the warmth of our
history wash over me
I was there through her most shattering moments
She came through to show support in mine
And like a confession or prayer I formed the words
of my heart:
"I've missed you my friend."

What Channing Tatum Taught Me About Beatlemania

See what happens is that it builds inside of you.
Like a little portal to a truth you never articulated before
The obsession, performance you have had to play every day of your life
Grace
Reservation, and
Ladylike behavior
Is now instantaneously in serious doubt
Perilous danger of becoming fleeting and potentially disappearing altogether
In the face of such rare beauty
Like a little secret joke that no one fully gets
No one else can fully understand
Eyes wide with anticipation and adoration at the object of your celebrity affection
Is it adoration?
Not sure but damn it feels good.
At first you become diminutive and quiet because you need to hear clearly the dialogue in your head
A wordless conversation of fiery hot adjectives and imaginative scenarios where you are the co-star

This vision that scrambles your reason and pulls at your core
Magnetism strong, mighty and comforting
Almost a giggle but becomes a growl when our mouth actually opens
Do you know what I'm talking about?

So this is what happened to those girls I saw
On that black and white footage on tv
So long ago
Swept up in a phenomenon called BEATLEMANIA

They saw the coy grins of the fab four with their slick suits
Suits that showed so much more than a teenage girl might imagine
See I don't think they had ever seen a clearly defined
Butt
Before they came on the scene
The Beatles were polished and sharp, yet rebellious with their hair that covered their ears
And dusted their eyes
Those dimples
And yes, that music
Completely, in every way

Unlike anything that they might see
In their every day
They were bad boys,
That these girls fantasized about
Longed to make room for in their structured
Pristine, chastity-belt ruled existences
Truly foreign, exotic, new and enthralling
And
They
Also
Had
Those
Accents
That promised a new way to pronounce the names
of every girl they were definitely going to marry
Or at least hold their hands, right?
And that is as far as it would go
Until the first girl slingshotted her bra up on to the
stage and it became a free for all
A vicious battle for attention to get the most
coveted of prizes
And the Beatles would sing, and smile those smiles
and shake those hips and sometimes make eye
contact with an Adoring fan
Triggering a tsunami of hormones and excitement
Accelerated, ignited
A primal chain reaction in teenage hearts

And all the girls would swoon
Exclaim
Hyperventilate
And lose their damn minds
Totally embarrassed, unable to control their own bodies and what reaction they would have next.
Some screamed until they had no voice
Pleading for release
Some clawed at their faces in a rush of emotion
Orgasmic like. The blood pressure would spike as the boys sang that part they loved so much
That one line that was their favorite. That release and rush of hearing it live
A moment like no other
Their bodies would fail them and some would literally pass out
Those sexually repressed girls were ready to riot just to get a glimpse of those Liverpool loverboys.
I don't judge them

Hell, they needed something to keep them warm at night
Something so rare, so unlike their regulated, suburban existence might actually offer

Funny

Right?
I always thought BEATLEMANIA was
So
Odd

Between you and me, I love live music.
Many, many times, I have had that musical climax
where you
Wait all night to hear
Your
Favorite
Song
Ever
And it is played just right
And the phrasing is perfect
And the guitar player makes that orgasm face when killing that solo or the drummer plays the shit outta that thing until your heartbeat matches the moment.
Fucking delicious

My life has had some serious thrills. Moments of pure ecstasy
No matter what, I could always keep it controlled.
Play it cool and not get star struck
I could always keep it contained
Rationalized even
That is, until Channing Tatum came along

Curious as always, I ordered a movie on demand called *Magic Mike*.
What
Is
Happening?
That smile, those eyes
Dear god, those lips
And yes, that body
What?
What?
A man so beautiful, he made Matthew McConaughey seem more like a distraction
Instead of the star attraction
Matthew was supposed to be
Allright, allright, allright
But this child takes the stage in a dramatic fashion
Striking one of those Atlas-like poses
And begins to dance
Can I even call it dance?
It was movement so fluid, so unreal that I sat there slackjawed at the transitions
Hardcore athleticism
Incredible artistic talent
Unlike those bachelorette parties where
Some oiled up musclehead would flip you upside down and whack you in the face with their obvious

Costume

Accessories and additions

And you cheered, smiled, made it rain and went along for the ride with your girl because it was

Her

Night

Out

Her chance to be a "bad girl."

Yawn

But Channing,

Chan, as I like to call him

Articulated

As he would glide across the stage

Doing acrobatic Kama Sutra moves

To sultry soundtrack

Literal feats of strength

Gyrated

Simulated

A pressure point is touched somewhere in my brain and I became fixated on his smile, pursed lips.
Did I mention his lips?
Even his damn calves somehow have a seductive glow that I never paid attention to before.
My mind blown, racing, traveling at warp speed through a million fantasies and

Imagined scenarios with me as the co-star, of course.

Dear god, he is perfection

And I find myself screaming at the tv
No cool
No control
Some fucking weird amalgamation of lust
Obsession and mental overload takes over
And I am screaming because it is the only right thing to do
The only thing to do
The only way to release
The stress of work, the monotony of adulting
I seek an escape that at the moment feels
Damn good
And my shame at my response
Should make me retreat into embarrassed girly giggles
But instead...I just want to keep   fucking
          screaming
I want to destroy his wife
I want to start a riot for *my* chance to see if fantasy is anything like reality
Even just a little bit
I will settle for a taste

As soon as I stop screaming

Because I am actually star struck by Channing Tatum

In all his beauty

And even if they come out with a Magic Mike Part Three

I will not be signing up to be an extra

In that cinematic masterpiece

Because I have already proven

That I have a hardcore case of

CHANNINGMANIA and will likely

Just scream in his presence

And

Never

Stop

Just like those girls I saw in the black and white footage on tv

Fargo

Fargo, North Dakota is a bizarre place
Really
Not much more needs to be said then that sentence.
But, I will say it again:
Fargo, North Dakota is a bizarre place.
This cold city in the middle of somewhere
Where they do actually talk like Francis McDormand did
They made "You betcha," a thing long before Sarah Palin came on the scene.
I was but a teenager, so far from home
On a school trip where anything can happen
Far from the eyes of anyone who could judge me
I could go anywhere, wander the streets.
Well, sort of.
See they have lettered half-streets there.
No, not shortened blocks or pedestrian alleyways
But honest to goodness half-streets.
An indecisive infrastructure that is yet totally appropriate for this place.

Fargo
Is where I no longer wanted to be stuck in between childhood

And adulthood.

Where I saw that number line and no longer wished

To remain on some marker

In between two wholes while I felt only half.

In Fargo, I wore lots of makeup

Push up bras and cleavage

Tight pants and cute boys everywhere

I was determined to have adult experiences

But really, I was just a kitten

And a clumsy one at that.

Meow

I spent a great deal of time studying

The person who would be "the one."

The person who would have the chance to

Make a woman out of me

Whatever that was supposed to mean.

It had to be someone that I would never see again

But could deliver an experience

Just like in the movies.

In the movies, women knew just how to act

And men understood them clearly

So clearly

But these were not men

And I was not clear

But I was bold

And foolish

So

I
Sought
Him
Out
Funny, attractive, talented with a
Naughty sense of humor
I made a point to hang out near him
Lean in close
Bat my lashes and laugh heartily at his jokes.
I imagined his lips inviting me
In,
His hands guiding me
On to the next phase
But I had to let him know
He was the
Chosen
One.
In the movies,
Grown-ups did bold things to communicate sexual desire.
Succeed or fail, I was determined to try some of those things.

Newly inspired by Michelle Pfeffer's super sexy, performance
As the one and only Cat Woman

I drew Cleopatra eyes
Pumped Siouxie and the Banshees in my walkman
And cobbled together my sexiest version of a catsuit
Sidled up to my mark
And ordered a milkshake
Strawberry
With extra whipped cream
We went through our usual exchange
Joking about our day
I turned my best
Flirt
On
Playing coy
Crinkled nose
Toothy grin
Kitten purr
Then leaned in close
And whispered in his ear
"I would love to get to know you better,
Meet me in my room tonight."
And like that, I slipped my hotel key into his coat pocket.

I left feeling a rush
Excited, emboldened and
Terrified
I went to my room

And waited

And waited

And waited

Feeling embarrassment

Horror

Shame

Maybe relief

That he did not take the bait.

But did that mean I was ugly?

Did he not understand my proposition?

The next morning

I emerged

Still a girl

Just a girl with dark makeup circles under her eyes

Back in my typical teenage costume

And he came to me.

He smiled and said,

"Do you want this back?"

And placed the key back in my palm.

Flush with shame

I couldn't speak or make eye contact.

"Let me tell you the truth,"

He leaned in, breath hot on my earlobe

Sending sweet shivers down my spine

"The truth is

Honey

I am

Gay."

He gave me a sympathetic embrace

And we never spoke of it again

And I returned home

From

Fargo, North Dakota

With my girlhood intact

Still just an awkward, foolish child.

Helpless Romanticism

All I Have to Give to You

Scrawled across the blank portions of the creased greeting card, these words were written and delivered in an envelope with my name across the width of its seal:

I want to give and give and give some more
Smother you with kisses and affection
Coat your thoughts with terms of endearment
And grand odes to your beauty
That playfully echo in your subconscious
And brighten your day

I want to share so much with you
Comfort you when you are weary
Please you when you are longing
Amuse you when you are bored
Be there when you need a compassionate ear

But what I really want to do
Is put my needs aside
And instead, for a moment
Focus on you
Whatever it is that you truly want
And deliver on every promise I make to you

You deserve all this and more

You deserve to receive and be fulfilled

You deserve all that I have to give

It's Not Enough

It's not enough that your words have captured my heart
That your desires speak so plainly and proudly
Declaring your wishes, fantasies and dreams of another time and place
Where our souls can roam freely, love deeply, give fully
Not bound by the constraints of convention and circumstance

It's not enough that I feel changed from knowing you
Challenged to unleash my imagination, my inhibitions

To give openly to a stranger without hesitation
Diving into the abyss with near reckless abandon
Praying for blissful continuance into perpetuity

It's not enough that we fit so well together
Mirroring thoughts and passionate dreams
Even though we come from different worlds
Different ages, different lifestyles, different cultures
Yet those differences always seem to disappear when we are in each other's arms

No

It's not enough

It's not enough

Indeed, it's so much more than I ever could have hoped for

Reveal

Emotions and sensations rush through my core
I find myself scintillated and stimulated
Invigorated and renewed

You inspire me

I put words onto the page that reveal
My desires, dreams and vulnerabilities
They pour from my fingers
And coat my thoughts like honeyed wine
Sweet and exotic, familiar and yet foreign
They intoxicate me and remove my inhibitions

I let my armor fall to the floor
Like rose petals
And I am left to face myself
Bare
Exposed

Through your eyes
I see reflected
The me
I truly wish to see
And for the first time
In a long time

I fall in love again with my complicated

Often misunderstood

Unconventional

Sometimes irreverent

But undeniably beautiful spirit

And I find my purpose once again restored

Teenage Love Letters

First Blush

Unnaturally angular shoulders formed by severe padding to draw our eyes away
From the sleeves of dress jackets that were a little too long for the wearer
A perfectly placed single Windsor-knotted tie atop a hand-pressed, starched oxford shirt
Safety pins stretched wide to mitigate the gap my fully pubescent cleavage wedged across buttoned blouses with lace trimming that caught many a roving eye
Runs in cheap hose, nude colors five shades off my creamy, ebony hue
Straightened hair neatly tucked into a tiny bun
Drug store makeup
My mother's pearl earrings and heels that hurt to walk in
We were children in adult adornments earnestly seeking validation and victory on any given Saturday
I was in your house, walking its halls, unaware of your legacy
An impish grin, firm handshake
Flaming red locs
Pale freckled face turned reddened warm

Nervous laughter, toothy grins
Breath suspended in my chest rising into my throat
I fell into the vastness of your eyes
My brow both arched in surprise and furrowed in confusion
At the range of emotions my mind held in a single moment
We found our footing and you led me to the arena
Now hypnotized by your charms
You mustered bravado and set to reign on that hallowed battleground
Emotion, skill, mastery of language and presentation
You fired a shot
I returned volley
I handily won
Humbled, awed, inspired you told me
And I believed you
That is where it all began
You offered up a glimpse into an abundant heart
Through unrehearsed love letters, you crafted phrases and stanzas that rocked me to my core
I asked for more and you gave without hesitation
The memories of which remain ever close
Your notes wrapped me in wonder of what the seemingly limitless world would have in store for us

Subtext and Secrets

Emerging from the dimly-lit stretch of the stairwell into the two or three-story walk-up, I slid in the back of the crowded room and took a seat well out of view.
This room filled with friends, neighbors, and acquaintances.

You flashed your smile, relishing the scene before you.

Dozens of members of your chosen family, crammed into a sweltering room with metal folding chairs placed into theatrical rows.
Whispering, tittering excitedly about the chance to hear you spill your secrets, bare your soul.
Each certain in their personal understanding and intimate knowledge of you.

I thought of the love letters and poems you wrote me a decade before.
I remembered the way your handwriting used to deliver words peace during my most confusing times,

When I questioned my own beauty, my worthiness to breathe and grace the world with my presence, You submitted me written proof of my silliness through each transcribed representation of your heart.

With my skin three shades too dark, my clothes still purchased on lay-a-way or from the Goodwill racks, my hair dull and intricately woven into hardened locs
My ass too big
My brain too large
My heart too vulnerable.

This room full of friends, neighbors, and acquaintances
Watched as you inhaled the admiration and opened your black book.

I knew well of the posture and the portal to your soul that would open and guide the letters to pour forth, form words and build a narrative
Each page another petal peeled away, to create a path to your center.
Spilling from your lips were the tender whispers of shared memories.
Gentle nods to a joke we crafted,

Stories that held echoes of some of our deepest pain and most formative traumas.
You created a touch that ushered direct connect to tears I had not met
And a vulnerability I wished to hide.
Did anyone know?
Could anyone tell?
The tune hummed beneath my tongue and the words swirled about:
"Strumming my pain with his fingers
Singing my life with his words
Killing me softly with his song, killing me softly with his song
Telling my whole life with his words
Killing me softly, with his song...."
I realize how quickly my own life might be laid bare and imbued into wrinkled pages of time.
It is an out of body experience.

This room full of friends, neighbors, and acquaintances rises to its feet
Proclaiming your genius to their delight.
Palatable as they embraced you.
Your proud face flush, shining, triumphant.
I patiently wait in line to greet you and
I touch my fingers to your cheek.

A warm blush as you sink into my affection and offer a loving smile.

I start to speak a voice cracked with suppressed emotion to whisper,

"I cannot share you tonight."

You smile empathically and nod in understanding.

I leave the bustle, descend the stairs and return again to the darkened streets where no one knows our stories

Forever changed and inspired.

Angel

One of the most exuberant parts of loving someone is the ability to trust them enough to allow them to rename you.
To select a name that holds the enormity of adoration and affection,
The utterance of which is hymnal to your heart.
You always greeted me as Angel.
The singular name for me that transcended decades, assures me that you still love me across spans of silence,
"Hi Angel,"
You said with a smile and grateful eyes.
And I knew then how much I longed to hear it.
Craved it. Needed it. Earnestly ached for it.
Still. After all these years.
It struck me hard, the truth that each time you call me by my given name
My heart still breaks a little because I know that I will have to wait for time to pass before I will feel the rush it brings again.
I want to hear it as a lullaby to comfort my weary spirit at the end of a trying day, soothing, secure and warm.
As a whisper to greet me in the morning

encouraging me to leap into the adventure offered in the day ahead.
To embrace my thoughts as I envision our revolution
As a reminder of my divinity, which you always revered.
And while it still hurts to tap into the memories of loss and separation,
To unlock those visages and moments with the simple incantation,
I could not imagine a life without its resonance.

Through the Darkness and into the Light

Anthem

"My, you seem angry," white supremacy says with a snarky, sadistic grin
As it presses its hand down on my face, smothering my protesting mouth, crushing my upturned nose and chin
"This is only the way business works
The business of world domination and
Your
Submission
Is just part of a system of manipulation to ensure that you remember your place in this nation
Where your citizenship is conditional
There are no true birthrights to respect, or acknowledgement of your humanity firstly
Because of your race
We owned you before you were born
A legacy and system that has never seen you as truly human
Equal to none and inferior to all
Inferior to all – your allowable presence is conditional. So don't tell me that your life matters girlie.
Because it doesn't."
"All lives matter," it says in an infantilizing tone,

"Not black lives. All - lives - matter. Because acknowledging your place in this world requires a recognition
Of a unique human experience that we determined is not worthy of notice.
How dare you even breathe with such grace?"
Each conversation must be heated,
dank
and
heavy in order to be legitimate
a true bloody battle of words.
I was once told that you do not have to attend every argument you are invited to.
So why is my existence the site of so much spiritual warfare?
"But we will never fight fair," it says,
We gleefully paint ourselves with your spilled blood as the victims
of *your* inherently evil ways
Your truth-telling
Your interruption to our superior trains of thought.
We will talk over you, dismiss your ideas and then repackage them as our own
As we are known to do.
Call it diversity and profit richly on your name."

"Your body fascinates

Erotic

Exotic."

"Sweet dark chocolate," is the pet name sexual exploitation gives me.

Dark and so different

To be readily consumed as a bucket list experience

No different than a trophy elephant

Slaughtered on safari

Splayed

Publicly displayed for pleasure and bragging rights

I know that I must use deliberate caution in my wardrobe

So as not to incite the imaginations

Of those who control the lens

The ubiquitous gaze

That lusts

And disgusts at my sight at the same time

The catcalls and the winks

The unintentional but blatant touches

The indecent physicality of everyday encounters

The loaded invitations to have "fun"

It is never actually rape because you wanted it

"In fact, you begged for it

With that round ass and sassy mouth of yours."

"Black women are insatiable and lascivious.

Your Africanness gives you the power of voodoo
and dark, magical seduction
Over lazy minds
We download your porn and obsess in our fantasy
but will deny any complicity
When grandma asks us who shares our bed.
Our women fear what you represent and wear their
insecurities like a badge."
A centuries-old jealousy burned into the DNA of
white women whose
Mothers
Watched
Their
Husbands
Rape
Take
and relish their dominance over women in the slave
quarters, harem halls, whore houses of the world.
"How dare you stand there in defiance and lack of
respectability in enjoying pleasure
On your terms?
Which part of objectification don't you get? You are
a toy. A plaything. A trending topic.
You are never to be trusted, but totally consumed
And then discarded into the periphery of history."

Corporate America chimes in with a sneer,
"And your hair is a little too revolutionary
Unkempt and so non-white"
The test has come, time and time again
That my promotions in my career
Synch perfectly
With the timing of when
I move away from black hair
To appropriate whiteness
I must prove my commitment
To become fully assimilated
To ascend beyond

All of my hard work and accomplishments are still beholden
To the whims of
Someone else's grace and
Willingness to give me what I have damn well earned.
I live in liminality, never secure that
I fit their twisted vision of whichever tribal/team fit/culture exclusionary human resources catch-phrase of day dictates my professional marginalization.
I just keep demanding acceptance into the places they tell me I don't belong.

The gatekeepers hold tight the keys and smile in your face as they are trained to do
And review the terms of agreement that state
"You deserve but a penance and will accept far less until you prove your worthiness to enter again and again and again.
You will do more. Make a way from no way and absorb the psychic baggage and physical destruction that exclusion causes. You have been breed through slavery, unnatural selection,
To have a superhuman ability to endure way too fucking much.
You will dance. You will produce.
Until your body collapses and your fingers bleed from the sweat equity of the
Black American Nightmare."
And I pull the food from my child's mouth to pay the exorbitant financial price of admittance
Promised through degrees, accreditations, professional development and deeper levels of commitment than others are expected to give.
It was all conditional.
It was all laid out in legalese, I just didn't read between the lines of the fine print in the social contract over my life. I trusted in the goodwill of the

powerful and privileged and now I am left spent, crushed and quivering.

I fight back with the strength of a hundred dark-skinned queens who held their tongues when they were called
"pretty for a black girl"
I speak louder with the conviction and ferocity of a thousand servant women who were told they were poor because they were lazy
I blatantly call out systems of oppression with the tactical acuity of women warriors like Nzinga, Tubman, Nanny and Shakur
And they turn on me
They scream curses for disrupting their ignorance
They join in unison to say,
"Foolish girl, it isn't us
It's *you* who has the problem
Your truth has wounded our pride
And *you* need to make us whole again."

I fight back tears
Exhausted from so many daily battles
Tired and worn
My defeat is what they want
My acquiescence is what they need
To put things in their rightful order

But I cannot be beaten unless I accept it
I know that I must rage against this machine

No longer a conscientious objector
To participating in this war
These ongoing battles for my soul
Here and now.
And the agony that is contained within cannot be held back
I feel the dignity of my foremothers being pulled out of whack
My spine stacked high with historical memories of warriors and goddesses who bowed to no one

Thus begins my transformation to my authentic self.

My skin tears at the graceful mask I wear when I need to hide
Scraped off in desperation to expose raw flesh
And complete lack of natural pride
As the blood rushes forth
My cheeks hot and reddened
My teeth grinding and clenching, gnashing and gnawing
The pinpoint precision of the drum cadence of my heart pounding through my temples

Eyes tired and weary stinging, screaming reddened and
Full of fiery rage
Singing to the tops of my lungs
Anthems to freedom
To rejection of bullshit
To empowerment
Hot, long and hard
For hours. Hours on end.
Tears.
Blinding tears, thousands of years in the making
For hours on end.
Until my throat cinches up like a vice
My body in all-consuming agony
And there is nowhere left to go
Other than to leave this fallacy
More final than a divorce
I look at my complicity in fostering this repression
See the carnage brought through this oppression
I reflect on the photo album of my life memories
And I realize that my smile has always been half measured
There for the moment but not real
And it all
Becomes
Too
Much.

I reject the notion that this relationship has ever worked for my benefit.
I will call you out by name, with no terms of endearment or forgiveness
Racism, misogyny, white supremacy, capitalism, bigotry, rape, exploitation and all of your relatives in your blood-stained family tree.
I see you clearly for who and what you are.
And I say to you
In a loud, clear voice:
No matter what you say,
No matter how clever the lie you tell,
It was you all along.

I will not leave this legacy to my children.
I will not place this imprint on future generations and make them
Think for even a moment that this has to be their truth.
Their life.
My life is mine to create.
And I will rise.
I'm done.
I'm gone.
Goodbye.

I Saw The Places They Died
(Honduras & El Salvador)

Special Note

I am so honored to have this poem entered into the United States Congressional Record by Senator Patrick Leahy of Vermont following a live reading of this piece on a visit with Oxfam America in December of 2019. Here is his beautiful introduction:

(12/12/2019)

TRIBUTE TO KIAH MORRIS [1]

Mr. LEAHY. Mr. President, I recently had the pleasure of meeting with my friend, former Vermont State Representative Kiah Morris, who among many distinctions was only the second African-American woman ever elected to the Vermont Legislature. Kiah's talents are far-reaching. She has also been an actress of stage, film, and television, spoken word performance, as a singer, dancer, and arts manager. Whether as a legislator or on a theater stage, Kiah's work has focused on amplification of the voices of oppressed people, on human rights, and on social

---

[1] "Tribute to Kiah Morris (CREC 12-12-19)"*Congressional Record*" (2019) p. S7023-S7024. (Text from: *Congressional Record Permanent Digital Collection*); Accessed: December 30, 2019

justice. It was in keeping that Kiah recently traveled to El Salvador and Honduras under the auspices of Oxfam America to meet with families struggling with the violence, poverty, lack of opportunity, injustice, and hopelessness that is causing thousands of destitute, frightened people to abandon their homes to seek refuge elsewhere. In those countries, Kiah saw where people had been gunned down, victims of gangs or corrupt police. She listened to the stories of threats and extortion, of kidnappings and deadly attacks, of fear and desperation. Inspired by the people she met and outraged by the brutality they described, she wrote a poem. I ask unanimous consent that Kiah's poem, which captures the essence of what the debate here over Central American refugees should be about, be printed in the RECORD. There being no objection, the material was ordered to be printed in the RECORD, as follows:

I saw the places they died
I saw the places they died
I saw the blood on the wall as if it were fresh
I saw the bullet holes pierce their flesh
I saw the places where they died and their spirits left their bodies onto a heavenly place

Far from a war-torn country of our design which orchestrated their demise
On the darkened brick walls splashed with stucco
Metal bars on windows each home a fortress from the violence that hovers in wait across the thresholds
Street vendors who compete for our Starbucks money to feed their souls and nourish their bodies
I saw the places they died in the tears behind the eyes of a priest who saw too much
Mental memorials to the expressions of horror and sadness on the face of a mother who died trying to save their daughter's life
Their state-sanctioned murders to leave no witnesses behind
Ordered bullets to fillet her face so that no one might recognize their own mother's eyes in her frozen gaze
I saw the places where they died, where the children were not spared
No life too precious to halt corruption and gang warfare
Daily genocides where there are no sacred spaces or places to hide
I saw the places that they died in the cobblestone streets
And people are pawns in a corruptors endgame

The depth of the violence bears no shame
I saw the places where they died when I heard the women speak of the terror that they face every day
Every week
The normalcy of rape, the dignity decimated, the beatings meant to break and the constant earthquakes that shake the fragile state
I saw the places they died in the hopeful smiles of the proud feminists who carry the burdens of their sisters as a shield
To protect the dignity of their humanity which too often is forced to yield
I saw the places they died, float off into still air
Laden with promises unfulfilled and hidden ambitions laid bare
I craft petals with poem to form a bouquet dropped off in a history of genocide with the hope the path these roses display will propagate a garden in honor of the many places they died

For Clementina, La Lenca
(El Salvador)

She entered the dialogue
Like a rush of wind carrying stories that only remain
in the woven threads of the traditional garments
sold to touristas on the side of dirt roads
Each handcrafted flower and colorful flourish the remnants
Of a tongue she never knew
But a presence that demanded visibility
In one breath they said
No one remained
Their presence reduced to a spectral chapter
From which the audience was too inept to acknowledge
She made it clear
She is here, she lives, they live
And the tears flowed
Like the cleansing rain that washed our clumsy
footpath carved in blood and colonial mentalities
That linked her world to mine
Her lineage to mine
They call us Mestizo, Mullato, colored, other
We are here
We have always been here

Choosing Battles

Coiffed, customized, called by my celestial name
I stepped out into the darkness of the cityscape with its shadowed corners and bass beats
I rode in the back of the cab nervous and slightly terrified
I traveled alone and moved in faith that I would feel secure and protected at my destination
A reunion of friends a decade in the making
A respite from the daily attempted assaults on my womanhood and my blackness
Those with clear, malicious intent
To dehumanize me, create me as one dimensional, a caricature, a stereotype
Or declare me as dangerous, volatile and foreign
Claiming I had harnessed the power of the sun and moon set to detonate and destroy all I touch

I rode in this bumpy, crowded chariot as it swerved, bobbed and snaked to deliver me to you
A warm, nervous smile and embrace that sets my heart at ease
Generous laughs and welcomes into the sanctum
Musical notes and rhythms taking us to church
Heads bobbing, careful study of mastery unfolded

I saw pulsing auras and angelic wings
I begin to breathe

Needing nothing more than the moment to fill my
soul imbibing on bass licks and syncopations
There for my pure enjoyment and nothing else
matters
I feel lifted, covered by light and love
There is trust, comfort and the return of joy

Then without warning, the air shifts to an icy chill as
I am shunted to a lower station
Held at bay, mired in place
I declare my divinity and rightful passage
My words breed mockery as drunk, white men
encircle me
My poems and stories all now sound silly
Ridiculous
Foreign
Empty
And I see myself in their eyes, the image of a fool
No one worthy of notice
Humiliated and indignant, an ally emerges and
advocates for my acceptance into this falsely
privileged circle

I breathe as I find the face of a friend who pulls me
in close and embraces me deeply offering the
welcoming I truly deserve
It is lovely, and warm
Comforting and gracious
Lifting and amusing
I step back into myself and start pulsing my warmth
and laughter into space
Circling the room, I share a moment of vulnerability
and revelation with another spirit, fragile and also
forced to the periphery
As we bond, I see the coming storm reflected in the
glassiness of her eyes and the weariness of her
smile
We were both strangers in this space who would
soon enough be forced into expulsion

I had long learned the majesty of my own radiance
and the real danger that comes from being so
noticeably visible in spaces of darkness
This night would test the limits of that danger

Suddenly, the doors blow open and I am knocked
back by a cold breeze of contempt, insecurity and
power which steals all oxygen

A vibrational shift occurs, like tectonic spiritual plates slammed together
As the faces of the Stepford wives and wannabe Instagram celebrities formed ranks and made it clear that
I
Was
Unwanted
I saw her smile fade as the isolation mounted on the back of my new friend
She too was shunted, demeaned and disregarded in a room full of basicness and white girl, clique crew level arrogance
She shuts down her questioning mind with any substance that might numb her to the blows they mounted with their icy stares and physical fortress walls formed by flat, Gap khaki covered asses

I looked at her fading light and knew I could not be the safe harbor she needed
I could not take her with me
I saw her heart break into a million pieces all at once

She pleaded for help that I could not provide as I was too weak to fight back and did not want to

allow my rage to devise a precariously ungraceful retreat
I reeled from the intensity of anguish she shared in that moment and it was was too much to bear

Her tears soaked my stiffened shoulders as I said my goodbyes and began to my own path of self-preservation and healing
A fleeting moment of little notice to few if any that night that held significance
These words are the only testament to our shared pain that remained and my determination to rise above it all and let the music fill that emptied space in my heart

I Got Ex Issues

Heart Chakra

The saddest realization

Acknowledgment

Understanding

Reckoning

Admittance

Validation

Summation

Revelation

Of the trauma I had endured

Came from the cautioning of a healer

Who told me that

My heart chakra was closed.

This abundantly loving heart had shut down and gone dark.

I was so numb to my pain that I turned off my own pulse.

What an abomination.

Don't be amazed by how brightly I shine again after I pull the deadened layers away.

Just be ready to bask in all its glory.

Redemptive Entry

I remember the weapons of war deployed on my sexuality with full clarity, stitched together through the agonizing passage of time.

Lips ordered to fashion a barrier designed to cruelly deny the exchange of the microscopic cellular transferences of ecstasy
The energy of which defines the majesty of a romantic caress. It was just sex.

The self-loathing that distorts the face into frown lines and pressed lips which hiss disdain in defiance of my unfiltered brilliance.

The impotence that affirms a man's insecurities and persuades him to destroy those gifts freely given out of an unrelenting fear.

The cowardice that trains his mouth to refuse the release of any utterances of love or meaningful affection. You are insignificant and unworthy.

                                      The steel surgical
                                      needle he drives in
                                      his anger clumsily

rips my sacred
tissue into lopsided,
jagged holes
drawing diseased
threads of
disrespect and
diminishment into a
crosshatched
pattern of semi-
permanence.
She screams in
terror as the red,
lace pattern is
speared repeatedly
with brute force
until the nerves
cannot regenerate
and subsequently
perish in blood-
soaked
degradation.

The microscopic tentacles of each synapse scorched
and withered in the infectious decay left by an
overprivileged, undeserving soul cruelly granted the
power to remake nature's most intricate designs

and highest purpose through their carelessness and abuse.

With torturous tension, I push forth a guttural, traumatic wail that transcends time and sings in broken, discordant tones about the living legacy of lust, obsession and addiction for the sexuality and autonomy of black women.

Societally sanctioned demands to violate our dark, succulent portal to
                                      the cradle of the
                          universe
where the stars were born and your purpose
was
designed
through each orgasm
and wave of divine worship
which emanated from my soul and those of women
before and after me
now being imprisoned.
The cycle continues through my narrative.

The heat and heaviness of my labia as it swells with anticipation for the seam to be torn, stitched together through years of pain and betrayal.

Promises to heal, care for and resurrect the deadened chakral center are placed into the heavens and redirected as sunrays into a cloaked space. The practiced words fall from his lips and I am angered at the notion of risking further harm to my soul through my careful consideration of these overdrawn pledges. He will have to attempt his atonement with no promises for forgiveness from me.

Limbs cemented in place that must now be coaxed into recognizing safety in the sensations, trusting the remnants of pleasure beyond a reproductive purpose.

Fingers slick and leathery from the lengthy labor of redemption
                        that grants provisional access
                  to places few prove worthy to witness.
She requires an ultra-tender manipulation so that the sealed, keloided flesh is reminded of its divine capacity for connectivity with astral planes and is soothingly massaged back into her unique tenderness.

She demands a loving warmth of breath and caresses and exaltations and confessions and whispered prayers to initiate the reddened scars to melt away and reveal the delicate tissue and the graciousness of my broken heart seeking to be reborn from this deeply scarred womb.

His calloused hands can only initiate this redemption, my soul will continue this work in her own time as a crucial part of my life's journey.

The Shadows Reflected In My Pupils

The parameters of delayed pleasure are vast
He held an image of me in his mind from my younger years when I wore my rebellion and individuality in my petite hands
Drawn on lipstick, and bare midriffs that revealed a belly-piercing with a daisy flower charm dangling from it, decorating my womb and sex

I wore lapel pins that were either a squiggle or sperm depending on your angle of observation.
Pinky rings that depicted couples entangled in simultaneous acts of oral sex
And I knew every erotic technique to be learned from Cosmopolitan magazine, Dr. Ruth and the *Joy of Sex*

I was careless and carefree, up for an adventure down for just about anything and anyone
Engaged in fucking that was still young and unskilled, my pleasure an afterthought or happy accident
I wanted to believe that I knew what an orgasm really felt like

He just wanted to get laid on a regular basis
There was no future with him, his temper, acidic tongue and dismissive nature was too restrictive for my emotive, effusive spirit

What should have been a simple goodbye became a living nightmare as our true selves were revealed and the illusions were rescinded

Emotional weapons were discharged which cut to the bone
I hated him for moving on ahead of schedule because it had been mere days, barely weeks between our tepid goodbye and his declaration of love to someone else
A woman the complete and total opposite of me in every way possible
Shit sex
Shit relationship
Shit ending
Holy shit
And now he seeks exoneration I cannot give him
Absolution, reparations for the harm he caused
The heartache and humiliation
The rejection of all that was good and uniquely me
He begs for a second chance, has waited nearly a quarter of a century just to see my face and observe

closely as to whether or not I smile at the sound of his voice

Or if a specter of the hurt still lingers in the recesses of my mind

And are reflected in the shadows of my pupils

He hopes that the magnetism of shared memories will draw my lips to his when we meet

The wounds too deep, he will be denied

AA_NA

I came to you raw and real
Open and honest
With the sun highlighting my every curve, wrinkle and freckle on my benevolent skin
That you swore wore an ethereal glow and abundance of divinity
Or so you said in moments of light and warmth
Until your words obscured, shadowed, dripped contempt and insecurity and incredulity
Flecks of blood-stained saliva, regurgitated conversations with past lovers
Propelled between clenched teeth shut hard from irrational fear, self-hatred and an alcohol-induced disease that has decimated your once beautiful mind
Each confession of drunken love followed by a tirade of repugnancy, explosive blasts
Rose up from your chest and projected shards of a fragile, long-broken ego to
Form a crown of thorns on my forehead
You looked to me to bear the burden of your sins and accept your whips and lashes
I am not a martyr but a woman with ancestral greatness
Worthy of adoration

See what I came to realize is that my face reminded you of your mother
And the girl you gave your first kiss to
My voice bore frequencies of the tune your first true love hummed, the melodies she sang as she planted rainbow-colored blossoms in the garden that first transformed your house into a home
My touch a swirling mass of deja vu from the discarded memories of fingertips snaked between the soft locks of your hair
Her gentle touch that calmed the pain of the world and the hauntings of your past enough to slow your breathing and soothe your restless heart after a weary day
Or her nails as they scraped along the width of your shoulders when her legs
My legs
My body
Pulled you close into sweat-laden embrace while the climaxes overtook again and again
The vibrations of fleeting ecstasy piercing your hardened spirit causing you to exclaim in amazement
All that she gave in the past thought forever lost, dumb luck returned to you ten-fold when you were least able to receive the gifts

Embodied in my presence
You remembered that you were born to worship and exalt but spent too many years neglecting your own calling
Drowned daily
Demanding that which was meant to be freely given if you were only willing to earn it
You tried to cheat the system by crafting a rich deception
Fantasy built on a million lies and blatant omissions
Wholly unnecessary in a place where truths are held sacred and your vulnerability would find safe harbor and perhaps even my heart
The guaranteed path to your fall from my grace began in the center of your self-inflicted loneliness
But again, I must remind you that I am not a victim of abusive love or hateful love or any other false names for actual love
I will not save you from your disease
Through grace, I come into light from your darkness healed, resurrected and shining my fullest glory
Never again to be eclipsed

The Politics of American Racism

When Picket Fences Feel More Like Barbed Wire Barricades

Capitalism functions by fooling the minds into believing the erroneous premise that the self is all that matters in life

Me

Mine

In

Out

Transactional and strategized to provide maximum gain for a singular someone, somewhere

The grotesque hoarding of moments, memories and minutes

The freedom of movement and identity

Belonging

Unconditional

Familial sense of community and togetherness

Got sold out for color-coded Google calendars

To define who shares minutes and seconds of this fleeting timeline for an unpromised future

We are set to teach our children the ways to be fully human

To love and appreciate their ability to connect with other beings
But choose to show them a micromanaged, over planned
Delineated model of friendship, family and community
So that children can only play between the hours of two and four
Or on a private swingset that only few ever get to enjoy
Tucked away in the back of someone's yard where the borders are legally defined and trespassing is a crime
These children must adhere to a strict schedule because folding laundry is more important than learning compassion
And bedtime routines are more sacred than any amount of unregulated play
Unbound
Imaginative
Mommy is too tired and daddy is too drunk and angry to let the boys find a moment of bliss
Away from the hard rules of their parents' privileged illusions of life, and
Mental messiness

Our children have not lost their natural ability to embrace the need for self-care
They intuitively know what they need to survive this inhospitable society
We are the ones needing guidance

My son plays with friends in his mind
Creates elaborate scenes for days at a time
With only the laughter and whimsy of his own voice to keep him company
Because he was never a part of someone else's suburban, white-washed vacation plans and exclusive playgroups that never have room or resources to include this beautiful brown soul
Who is treated more like an inconvenience and often an interloper to defend against
Instead of an actual fucking child

Bleached Bloodlines

You chose to hate me because someone told you that it would bring you
Peace and Joy
You decided to dehumanize me because there is a hole in your spirit, eaten away, scarred heavily from some heinous pain that burned away and erased your fingerprints
Made you forget your name as one of G_d's
Children
You gave your religion away to profit greatly
From demagoguery and false idolatry
You bleached your bloodlines until they ran clear from the amputated heritages
That marked you non-white
You re-wrote our history, placing blame on me and those who look like me and those who love me for the pains of your everyday
The harsh reality you now face that the American dream
Is at its roots a lie

Meant for the Slaughter

It is an odd sort of comfort one must find
In order to justify gross vilification and demonization
Necessary to the point where one can easily say,
"Well, not everyone agrees with her politics."
Or
That this is isn't about race, "it's about her personality."
And to allow that acerbic mirage to overtake your presumed intelligence and superiority to say
"This one is meant for the slaughter," the offering necessary to please the devil
So that your life can continue thriving off the sweat that drips from my brow, furrowed in disbelief that anyone can find themselves so far from godly.
"If she can be stopped, we can be returned to our blissful naivete and say that we gave it our best shot."
"If she can be buried, then our soil will be enriched with her tears"
"And all god's children say, 'amen.'"

Respectability Politics

How does one forgive what has not yet had the
Gift of time to rest and find safe distance
From the certainly unique vantage
Of the betrayal of trust that a million microaggressions and
Gaslit hopes for justice within a flawed system that should be far less antiquated and dogmatic in its protection of those under its care
To have usefulness in a constantly evolving modernity

They were clear in their positioning
They relished their power
Spoke words of vindication and dismissal
A refusal to move
A failure to acknowledge
Using their pulpits and podiums to lie
To defame
To cast doubt
To grotesquely exonerate their calloused decisions that placed my life in further danger
Made my family a greater target
Fed the machine of white supremacy

Now that the world has seen your works
You expect
That I will embrace you like a brother
Stand there and pretend that all is forgiven
On your timeline

The demand for law and order was given greater importance than my life

And centuries of injustice
Cannot be forgiven to appease your need for the perfect photo op
And well-crafted headline
My mother's tears echo in my head and ground me to my place at this moment in time
All is not yet healed

Spirituality Manifested

Exponential Love

"I can't help but trip and fall over your energy," he says in an exasperated but gleeful tone, each word delivered through sighs of ecstasy and surrender. "It just spills over and covers me."

That is how a lover once described my essence as I kissed and caressed his adoring face following a most rapturous joining of our souls.

This energy, this loving energy that rushed forth after being dammed up against its will out of preservation. Soaking our bodies, the sheets, the bed, the room, that space
With pure love.

Tired and worn from too many days witnessing too many man-made deaths. From the frontlines of the Sisyphean work he does every day to care for the world. He needed replenishing, and I needed releasing. He needed healing.
We all do from time to time.

I was born a healer. It is part of my unique purpose. So, I opened my wellspring of divine, fulfilling,

compassionate love to lighten his heart and sent him back out into the world to do more good.
This love.
His love.
My love.
My
Love.
Something birthed in my soul before I was even born.
Imprisoned in a physical environment so embattled and traumatized that it recoiled from its charge to nurture my body.

A woman's heart broken and discarded asked to create a most precious gift of love – a life, another loving spirit to share with the world.

This body would struggle care for the delicate child within, and the pain of the world would invade the protection of the womb and seek to destroy me.
A disorder, a deadly, but common black mother's prenatal disorder became the marching orders in a fight for survival for both mother and child.
A war between
Heaven
and

Hell.

The casualties could be exponential, only Grace could save us both.

The mixed signals told her body I was a foreign invader that was to be extinguished.
My spirit wrapped itself in a cocoon of love and light and held on to the promises of providence to survive the onslaught.

When nothing more could be done, both of us barely holding on to this plane,
We were pulled from the wreckage, mother and daughter separated for days, weeks, months to heal.

A delicate life seeking the physical comfort of her mother, her touch, my heart began to pulse out love songs to the universe.

My cries vibrated rhapsodic, loud and clear messages of love like a beacon in the vast isolation to draw others to my light.

Undaunted, unaware of my supernaturally small size, ignorant to the natural rules that empirically predicted me dead,

My voice would blast through the Plexiglas prison walls with resounding force.
Those who heard it believed it to be as the definitive hand of God touching their hearts, drawing them to me.

And I would give them my love. And their hearts would lighten.

And so it would go on into infinity, my mission to give mighty love, to love fully, freely, fearlessly.
"I love you," I would say to the nurse as she used scraps of fabric and napkins to swaddle my warm, miniscule body.

"I love you," I would say to my sisters who nearly lived their greatest fear as they watched their mother struggle to breathe, heart still shattered into a million pieces, too physically weak to comfort them or assure them in the way that mothers naturally do.

"I love you," I would say to my sisters' father upon his release from prison. His hardened face turned tearful as I wrapped my small fingers around the palm of his hand. His own daughters too stunned to articulate the fear and elation of having their father back in their lives again after so many years. I would be the conduit for their love.

"I love you," I would say to the boy from across the street when I used my body as a shield between him and the bullies who tortured him so much that he would wet his pants in fear. Even though his father called me a nigger.

"I love you," I would say to my friend's little brother every time I visited their home. I always sat down next to his wheelchair decorated with tubes and machines, conversing with a boy whose body robbed him of mobility and normal speech with every visit. We talked about the day, movies we loved, and Power Rangers.
He would laugh and smile
And his mother reflected her love in the warm tears that silently ran down her flush cheeks while she watched us.

"I love you" I said to my best friend as I held her tightly through wrenching sobs. My family was too poor to send me on the class trip, so I stayed behind and did busy work in a half-empty school while my friends were away. She told me about how they placed her in the same room as the rich, mean girls who mocked, insulted her and forced her to sleep on the floor. My love could not protect her from such cruelty.

"I love you," I said to my mother as I mopped her sweat-soaked brow. Once again, death would call her name but I cared for her through my fears and the painful battles with my sisters who still carried the ghosts of their childhood nightmares of losing her and directed their tears at me. She would pull through. That divine love healed her.

"I love you," I shouted as I waved goodbye to my ex. His deep, dark, unrelenting depression robbed him of his life, his ability to love and to see me. I gave and gave my love in a million ways, hoping that this love would make a connection, would overcome the ever-present adversity that obscured and destroyed our love. I was spent, depleted and undone. To love him, I needed him to find his own path. To heal myself, I needed to love myself enough to let him go.

"I love you," I whispered to our friend as he lay on his death bed, family too distraught to function, bereaved at the mere thought of his impending departure. Calm and steady, I comforted him and convinced him to accept the life-giving tube and to carry on until he was ready to don his angelic wings. He would steal another three Christmases and birthdays, long enough to ensure his daughter's eyes would be the final vision he carried with him to heaven.

I would repeat those words to my granddaddy during our final telephone conversation. I let him know that our love was eternal and that it was okay to rest and be free of pain. We would all be okay, I promised him. We would never stop loving one another.

I never fear loving or telling others that I love them as it is infinite energy. Transferrable energy. The natural order. I wrap my love around my son, pledge my love to my partner, share my love with my work and my art, nurture my love with my family, exemplify my love with my friends. But most importantly, honor that my love

Never
Belonged
To
Me.

It is but on loan from God, and with this poem, I now give this love to you. Please use it generously.

Greatness

Greatness is not a destination

But a dream manifested

Through the blood, sweat, and tears

Of the brave and the generous

Who expose their beating hearts to the world

The cadence of which synchs

With the earth's sobbing

And the vibrations of which become a meditation

The colors and shapes that declare our Universal Ancestry

The ultimate embrace of one's divine purpose

Kaleidoscopic Transferrence

Peering down the corridors of destiny, I catch a glimpse of honesty
An illuminated soul glides across my path, shining wisdom, grace, and genius
I watch with curiosity and wonder to see so many
Eager, hungry hands clumsily grasp at the glow they give only to feel it slipping through their outstretched fingers

Despondent
They fail to see the new, brilliant colors that they temporarily
Create from the blending of their lights

I enjoy the kaleidoscopic swirling of warm tones and sharp hues that are captured as they move onward

Reaching towards the light, I catch contact with the source
Memorize the patterns and move onward to continue the cycle with another who seeks
And wants the same

Natural Giver

When one is a natural giver
It can be hard to receive
A new skill that has to be honed
Like learning a new language
Or building a natural palate
For a somewhat foreign taste

Opening oneself up to the possibility
Of feeling the return
Knowing the bliss
Understanding the gift
Accepting the responsibility
Recognizing the sanctity of
Love rebounded and doubled exponentially

Letting loose our need to control
To protect
The source which feeds
Our giving
Becomes essential
When faced with the undeniable truth
That we all are indeed
Deeply
Loved
And were in fact born

For the purpose of
Living a life full of
Loving reciprocity

About the Author

Originally from Chicago, **Kiah Morris** lives in the Green Mountain State of Vermont where she served in the general assembly as a State Representative from 2014-2018. She was the first African-American and person of color elected from Bennington County and the second African-American woman to be elected to the legislature in Vermont history. Her story of success and struggle have been covered in over four dozen media outlets including CNN, The Huffington Post, New York Times, Washington Post, The Hill, Essence Magazine, Canadian Broadcasting Company, PBS, BBC Radio and Vice Media.

She is an award-winning, in-demand trainer, speaker and presenter. She provides consultative services, workshops and presentations on issues of diversity, equity and leadership for organizations across the globe.

Kiah also holds an accomplished artistic career as an actress of stage, film and television, spoken word performance, as a singer, dancer and arts manager. As an arts advocate with a passion for community-based art, she has produced numerous special events, concerts and art exhibits during her career. Her work focuses on amplification of voices of the oppressed, issues of human rights and social justice.

For bookings, please visit: Kiahmorris.com

Made in the USA
Middletown, DE
14 May 2023